A simple but effective guide
money management guide
for teenagers

Isaac N. P. Carter

LIFE AND SUCCESS PUBLISHING
www.abookinsideyou.com

Copyright © Isaac N. P. Carter 2010

All rights reserved. No part of this publication may be reproduced distributed or transmitted in any form or by any means including photocopying recording or other electronic or mechanical methods, without the prior written permission of the author, or except in the case of brief quotations embodied in critical reviews and certain other non commercial uses permitted by copyright law. For permission requests, write to the publisher, addressed

"Attention: Permissions Coordinator"

at the email address below

Life and Success Media Ltd

email: info@abookinsideyou.com

www.abookinsideyou.com

This publication is designed to provide accurate and authorative information in regard to the subject matter covered. It is sold with the understanding that the publisher is not engaged in rendering legal, accounting, or other professional service. If legal advice or other expert assistance is required, the services of a competent professional should be sought.

ISBN: 978-1-907402-93-7

Cover design and layout by Natasha Williams

CONTENTS

Acknowledgements 5

Foreword 9

Introduction 11

It's Never Too Early! 15

Financial Institutions 19

Rules Of Financial Management 25

- ☐ you never spend more than you have.

- ☐ Save Save Save Save

- ☐ Avoid getting into debt

- ☐ Educate Yourself Financially

- ☐ Develop A Financial Mindset

Money Management For University Students 41

The End 47

A Note To Parents 49

ACKNOWLEDGEMENTS

Thanks to:

Beverly Hendricks for planting the idea of GT2A in my head. My teen focus group made up of my Son (Isaac Jnr), my niece Jasmine Carter-McDonald, Toni "Ant" Titus, and Rachel Melton, who all brought a healthy dose of realism to my initial draft of this book.

To Len Allen, who is not only a great mate and mentor but is also a constant source of challenge and inspiration.

Finally and most importantly, my Wife Pauline Carter (my peanut) who continually supports and reminds me that I can do anything I put my hand to.

Take a lesson from the ants, you lazybones.

Learn from their ways and become wise!

Though they have no prince or governor or ruler to make them work, they labour hard all summer, gathering food for the winter.

<u>Proverb</u>

FOREWORD

From the day you were born money has been playing a very important role in your life. As a matter of fact, even before you were born money was spent preparing for your arrival, then celebrating your birth; buying clothes, gifts, toys, and more importantly providing a home for you.

Money pays for your education, your leisure, food and shelter; in fact more or less everything you do requires money in one form or the other.

So we see money is important; but if it's so important surely we need to understand how we can make more of it, manage it effectively, and consequently keep more of it.

It is a known fact that if an employee earns just £30,000 per year for an average working life of 35 years he or she will have made over £1,000,000 in their lifetime, yet most people end up broke. So if you are going to be successful in life with money management, it's never too early to start, and here is where we start. So let's get to work!!

INTRODUCTION

If you are between the ages of 13 and 18 (or over and in full time education) you need to read this book because it contains information that you desperately need.

For reasons best known to themselves those in power with the responsibility of providing your life education, as opposed to academic qualification have seen fit to educate you about wars that took place hundreds of years ago, and countries you may never visit, whilst at the same time depriving you of the basic knowledge required to understand how the financial system in this country works.

One of the greatest puzzles of the modern education system in the United Kingdom today is the reluctance to make it a legal requirement for schools to teach pupils about the source, use, and value of the currency of the realm, in other words, **MONEY!!**

Without any information, education and preparation, your generation is doomed to make the same mistakes as the previous ones, falling into debt, living on credit, having no savings and ending up broke.

In **Go 2 the Antz** we want to start right now by informing and educating you about the basics of managing your money by looking at:

- how money operates in our society,
- how financial Institutions work

- ☐ How you can develop good habits of money management in your teenage years.
- ☐ How you can be money Smart
- ☐ Why you should save
- ☐ how to increase your financial intelligence
- ☐ Why it's not too early for you to start your own money making ventures.

Finally I know you're thinking what has all this got to do with the Ant? Well here are five main characteristics of the Ant which you need to adopt in dealing with your money:

The Ant is:

- ☐ Future focused
- ☐ Organised
- ☐ Industrious
- ☐ Never gives up

These are the qualities you need to bring to your understanding of managing your finance.

How to get the Most out of this Book

This is a practical book or what you might call a "how to" book so we can walk through it together, step by step, ticking off each point and going through each stage until we reach our final destination.

The best way to get the most out of this book is as follows:

- **Take your time:** Please don't rush! Read each chapter thoroughly, make notes and then follow any instructions set out in the chapter before moving on.

- At the end of each chapter there is a summary and a few questions on its contents. **Follow each step carefully before moving on**; this way you will see the actual progress in what you are learning.

- Use this book as a working tool and as it helps you, use it to help your friends; better still, recommend they purchase a copy of the book.

Now, if you are a teenager read on. **If you are an adult pass this book to a teenager!!**

Chapter 1
IT'S NEVER TOO EARLY!

There is an old song called "Money makes the World go round" and this to a large extent is true.

Put at its most basic, money is what we exchange for goods and services in our society today. Be it sterling (England), dollars (US), yen (Japan), or the Euro (Germany), the likelihood is that if you want something you are going to pay for it with money. Clothes, food, shelter, leisure, entertainment and travel are all every day goods and services which we all use, and to access them you have to use money.

You may be thinking why is this book written for teenagers, surely at this age I don't have enough money to be worried about financial management, think again. Do these names sound familiar?

- ☐ Nike, Timberland, Adidas, Rocawear; these are clothing retailers whose products are targeted primarily at young people.

- ☐ Nickelodeon, Bravo, MTV, and many other TV channels and PC down-loads for young people.

- ☐ T-Mobile, Orange, Vodafone, 3, and O2; all phone manufacturers churning out new models at an amazing rate with ever increasing levels of technology.

- ☐ Finally, the gaming industry with PS3, X Box, and Nintendo Wii

They are all targeting you!

The truth is that the youth and teenage market in this country alone is worth over a **£2.7 billion.** All the retailers, phone companies, and game manufacturers have one thing in common--they are all targeting you; telling you what to buy, how too look, what to wear, and what to listen to. They know the youth and teenage market is huge and they are dedicated to targeting you and **your money!!**

So obviously, somebody thinks you have money and the truth is you do! It may be your allowance, pocket money, money from relatives, money from your part time job, or more than likely from the Bank of Mum and Dad but wherever it's coming from you're spending it, and probably even without thinking about it. And that's the problem!

Now don't get me wrong, there is nothing wrong with spending money, but if you learn the habit of how to spend money without understanding its value, or how to manage it at this early age when you have a limited amount the chances are that as you get older and get more money you will keep on behaving the same way, and trust me that is not good.

<u>Summary</u>

1. **Money is the currency we exchange for goods and services**

2. **As a teenager your money is important and there are retailers which specifically target teen expenditure**

3. **The teen market in the United Kingdom is worth £2.7 billion**

<u>Task:</u>

Make a list of the things you spend your money on.

Chapter 2
FINANCIAL INSTITUTIONS

Before we embark on any discussion of money management you must first have an understanding of the financial institutions which operate within the United Kingdom today. Barclays, Nat West, HSBC, Nationwide, Santander; these are all names with which you are probably familiar and are all well known financial institutions; they are not however identical. Financial Institutions can be separated into 3 groups:

Banks

HSBC, Barclays, Lloyds TSB and National Westminster are what we refer to as the "Big Four" because they are the most well known banks and have a presence on most high streets. Banks have a number of functions but their main business falls into 3 basic areas (i) lending money to individuals – residential (ii) lending money for investment in businesses/purchase of commercial property (iii) investment in shares and commodities through the stock market (a financial trading market where financial markets throughout the world can buy and sell shares). They also provide credit cards, car loans etc.

There are many other commercial or investment banks but for the purposes of this book we will concentrate on the Big Four.

Building Societies

Yorkshire Building Society, Nationwide, Bradford and Bingley, and Northern Rock are probably the most well known building societies in the United Kingdom today. Like Banks they have a very high profile on most high streets. They also have a variety of functions like banks, however, the majority of their business is made up of providing saving, investment, and lending facilities to individuals to buy residential properties. They also provide small loans to buy cars, and credit card facilities.

Finance Companies

Finance companies are less well known and are usually used by individuals only after they have used either of the above two. Ocean Finance, Wellcome Finance, GMAC. These companies are finance companies which do not have a high street presence like banks and building societies but provide a secondary level of finance for individuals due to the high rates of interest they charge (see chapter 3 below). They also offer loans to buy houses and cars.

Sooner or later, you will end up having dealings with some or all of the above financial institutions and it is therefore important for you to understand how they

FINANCIAL INSTITUTIONS

work if you are to be successful in understanding money management.

Most importantly you must understand that financial institutions exist solely for the purpose of making money; which they do primarily through investment, lending, and borrowing. A major tool in the bank's box of tricks is interest.

Interest

As we have already said, above all, financial institutions make money through lending which is a huge part of their business to companies, institutions, and individuals. Lending is essential to financial institutions as they make money by charging interest on the money they lend. Interest is essentially a fee charged by the Financial Institutions for lending the money based on an agreed rate of percentage on the overall figure over an agreed period.

Fig 1

Bank lends Mr. A £1000 at a rate of 10% per year (APR) the total amount repayable is as follows: £1000 x 10% = £1100. So at the end of the year Mr. A will repay the bank £1100 which is made up of the original £1000 plus 10% of the £1000 borrowed which is £100.00.

Fig 2

However, if the same £1000 is lent over a period of 2 years then the interest charged in the second year will be on the increased figure of £1100 not the original £1000. The total amount payable is now therefore calculated as follows: £1100 x 10% = £110, which means the total amount repayable, is £1210. In other words the interest of 10% makes the bank £210.00 simply for lending the original £1000.00.

What is happening is that the borrower is paying interest on interest; this is known as compound interest.

So you can already see how profitable lending is for banks and how difficult it can be for the person borrowing depending on how much they borrow.

If you apply the same principle to credit cards, loans and mortgages, where the sums involved can involve hundreds of thousands, or even millions of pounds, you can see how financial institutions make a great profit out of lending.

From the above you can also see how important it is to ensure that you borrow only at a level you can afford and always check the interest at which you are borrowing.

In chapter 4 we will talk a bit more about this.

Borrowing

As well as lending, financial institutions also make money by borrowing money; that may sound surprising but they do it for a number of different reasons:

Firstly, to reinvest, sometimes even just overnight, secondly to lend to others at a higher rate of interest than they have borrowed, and thirdly, just to maintain the amount of money they have available. Banks will borrow from other banks or Governments but sometimes they borrow from you, yes you!

When you put your money in the bank you are lending it to them and they pay you interest on the money you lend them. Obviously, the more you lend the bank the more you get paid in interest; although this is partly dependent on the terms on which you lend to them (see chapter 3 on saving).

Not surprisingly the banks pay you a lower rate of interest on the money they borrow from you than the rate they charge you and it is important you understand this when borrowing money from any financial institution.

Summary

1. **The three main types of financial institutions are Banks, building societies, and Finance companies.**

2. **All Financial Institutions make their money primarily from (i) Lending and (ii) Investing**

3. **Interest is a fee charged by financial institutions on money lent to borrowers. The fee is based on charging the borrower a percentage of the money lent.**

4. **Financial institutions borrow money to (i) lend to others (ii) invest and (iii) maintain liquidity.**

Task:

Using the formula set out above work out how much Mr. A will pay if he borrows the sum of £5000 over the period of 5 years at a rate of 10% per year.

66% of Britons believe finance lessons would have helped today's financial challenges...

CHAPTER 3

RULES OF FINANCIAL MANAGEMENT

As a teenager you may or may not have a full time **income** as such, however you will have some income, whether it's from an allowance/pocket money (apparently the average pocket money paid to teenagers in the UK is £1000 a year), a part time job, student EMA (Educational Maintenance Allowance) or grant, even the Bank of Mum and Dad. You may even be running your own business (Richard Branson started Virgin Records at 16 years old from a BT Phone box and is now a billionaire).

If you are the average teenager you will most certainly have outgoings, maybe your mobile phone, your computer games, weekly lunch expenses, magazines and clothes. As we have already said, the teen market in the United Kingdom is currently worth £2.7 Billion.

So if you have income and outgoings, although you're not dealing with thousands of pounds, it is essential that you learn the principles of good money management so that when you really start earning and have more money you know how to handle it.

There are five basic rules of good money management that apply no matter whether you are dealing with £1 or a £1,000,000. Learn these and you are on your way to financial success in your future.

<u>**RULE 1**</u>

23% of teenagers tend to think of overdrafts as an easy way to spend more money than they earn...

The first rule of good money management is that <u>you never spend more than you have</u>.

If you spend more money than you have or make, you are in debt (see rule 3) and this is not good.

To ensure that you do not break rule 1 it's important that you keep track of money that you have coming in (income) and what is going out (expense). The tool we use to carry out this exercise is a budget.

Budget

A budget is basically a list which identifies all of your regular income and expenses and shows you how much money you have left after all your expenses have been paid. The aim is to ensure that you balance income and expenditure.

Examples of income:

(i) Pocket money or weekly allowance (ii) part time job, (iii) EMA (iii) Grant (iv)Student Loan

Examples of expenses:

(i) Mobile Phone, (ii) clothes,(iii) make up, (iv)magazine, (v) lunch, (vi) computer games, (vii) going out with friends.

A budget can be as simple or as complicated as you wish but it must list all your income and expenditure. It can be daily, weekly or monthly. It can be handwritten, on your mobile phone, your lap top, or your personal computer but once you have your budget you must stick to it.

In fig .1 below is an example of a budget, and on the following page is a blank form for you to create your own budget. Take your time and list all of your expenses; remember the list must be as detailed as possible.

Once you have finished these exercises you will have a much clearer picture of your financial state and be in a position to create your budget, which we will discuss in chapter 3.

When you have finished this exercise you can move on to rule number 2

Fig.1 BUDGET

INCOME	Date	£	
EMA		£	
Allowance		£	
Pocket Money		£	
Part-time job			£
Student Loan			
Grant			
EXPENDITURE			
Mobile Phone		£	
Leisure		£	
Clothes		£	
Trainers		£	
Cosmetics		£	
Lunch		£	
		£	
		£	
TOTAL			

Now try and create your own personal budget

RULES OF FINANCIAL MANAGEMENT

Fig.2 YOUR BUDGET

INCOME	Date	£	
		£	
		£	
		£	
			£
EXPENDITURE			
		£	
		£	
		£	
		£	
		£	
		£	
		£	
		£	
TOTAL			

RULE 2

54% of teenagers are interested in learning about savings...

Save Save Save Save

There is a famous saying that if you have a pound you can save 10p and this is true of all of us. It doesn't matter how much money you make if you can't keep any of it.

One of the most effective ways of keeping money is to save it. As with all the other rules in this book "it's never too early" to start saving. As a matter of fact, by the time you are reading this book you should already have savings of some sort, whether it's a savings account opened for you when you were first born or an account into which all your birthday money and special gifts go, you should have one.

Consider this, if you are now 18 and your parents saved just £10 a week in a deposit account since the day you were born you would now have a total of £9,360 and this is not including interest.

There are 5 reasons why you should save:

- **Money makes money** - As we discussed earlier when you deposit money with financial institutions they pay you interest just for saving it. The more you save the more you make thanks to the secret of compound interest.

- Compound interest is the interest you are paid on your original deposit plus interest. Therefore if you pay £1000 into the bank and get paid an annual interest payment of £50 then when your next payment of interest is payable it is actually paid on £1050 and not the original £1000 you deposited.

- From the above you can see how important compound interest is to your saving strategy and just how important it is, is shown by the **Rule of 72.**

- The **Rule of 72** basically states that in essence, the value of your money saved doubles every six years and the higher the rate you invest at, the quicker you can double your investment.

- **Saving helps you acquire the habit of using your own money for purchases** – Saving means that when you buy something it is bought with your own money. This is a good habit to acquire early and means that you will not get into the bad habit of borrowing or learning to depend on others; remember if you borrow from someone to purchase an item it is really theirs until you pay them back.

- **Save while you do not have to pay tax** – Everyone in receipt of income (including interest on savings) in England and Wales has to pay a percentage to the HM Revenue and Customs; this is known as **Income Tax**. As a teenager under 18, or a student in full time education, you are not liable to tax on interest paid on your savings; interestingly, you are also not liable to tax on earnings. So this makes it an ideal time for saving.

- **Save for the future** – It may seem too early to talk about saving for your future but depending on how old you are, having savings is always useful. Do you want to buy a PS3, x-Box or a new pair of trainers? If you are older you may be saving for a new car or University. Whatever it is you are saving for, the sooner you start the quicker and easier it will be to make your purchase. Again this is a good financial habit for you to acquire at an early age.

RULE 3

Over 50% of teenagers in England have been in debt by the time they are 17...

Avoid getting into debt

As we discussed earlier you are in debt when you are spending more money than you have. If your income from whatever source = x and your outgoings are y, which exceeds x you are living beyond your means and are in debt. This is a definite no for someone serious about managing money.

This is why it is important to keep a budget. Unfortunately, in the United Kingdom today, debt is amongst the highest in Europe with a large part of this being made up of credit card and loan debt. Although you may not yet be at the age where you have a credit card or can take out a loan it is still important that you understand what they are and the potential problems caused by debt.

A recent report from Credit Action showed that:

- Total UK personal debt at the end of March 2010 stood at **£1,460 billion**.

- **Individuals in the UK owe more than what the whole country produces in a year.**

- ☐ Total consumer credit lending to individuals at the end of March 2010 was **£222bn**.

- ☐ Average household debt in the UK is **£8,796** (excluding mortgages).

- ☐ Average household debt in the UK is **£57,950** (including mortgages).

In addition to the above figures it is important to note that in the United Kingdom many teenagers are also getting into debt from an early age. Sometimes teenagers get into debt using their parent's credit card. But with a large number of financial institutions offering student accounts for students in higher education, not surprisingly, there is a trend of ever increasing debt amongst teenagers.

Added to Student loans many teenagers are often struggling with debt by the time they enter adulthood and get their first jobs.

So what are the main sources of debt in the UK today?

Credit cards – are one of the main sources of debt in the United Kingdom today. A credit card is a facility which allows you to borrow money or buy goods up to a set figure on an agreed interest rate.

If the total amount borrowed on the credit card is not paid off within the time agreed (usually monthly) then interest is charged on the amount outstanding and continues to accrue on a compound basis until paid off.

Credit cards can be useful if paid off on a regular basis. Credit cards should never be used as a substitute for income or to purchase goods when you have run out of money and clearly have no means of repaying.

On a credit card you can in some cases be charged up to three different rates of interest:

- Rate for **purchase** of goods- this is usually the standard rate for the card.

- Rate for **balance transfers** (see below) – can vary depending on the deal you have been offered; can be as low as 0% in the initial transfer period but will rise to the standard rate once this has finished.

- Rate for **cash withdrawals** – this is usually the highest, and interest is charged immediately the cash is withdrawn with no interest free period.

There are some cards which offer an initial 0% rate for an introductory period or a balance transfer facility whereby, a debt from a card with a higher rate of interest is transferred to a card with a lower rate of interest; sometimes up to 8 months. These can, if used properly be a useful way of reducing interest payment on high rate cards but, again considerable discipline is required to take advantage of such a facility and to avoid ending up with a number of cards after the offers have expired with even higher rate interest on them.

Buy now pay later – this type of credit again offers you an initial interest free period when you can take the goods (car, furniture etc) without payment, and after that period is over you either pay one lump sum (inclusive of the rounded up interest) or effectively enter into a loan agreement.

Loans – Loans are a specific amount of money lent for a specific period at an agreed rate of interest. These can be used for purchasing cars, furniture, paying for holidays or paying off other debts.

It is important to understand from an early age that uncontrolled debt is the enemy of your financial success. Of course there are some types of debt which you may need, such as to buy a house in the future, but as a teenager you should strive to stay out of even the most minor amount of debt and adopt a principle of avoiding it at all costs.

<u>**RULE 4**</u>

Educate Yourself Financially
<u>**(Be Money Smart)**</u>

When it comes to money, ignorance is not bliss and what you don't know will hurt you. As important as the practical steps we have considered so far in this book is your personal financial education.

To develop your financial awareness you need to increase your education. I deal with sources of financial information and literature in the next chapter but, in this chapter we need to look at ways of increasing your financial education.

Poor money management and the resulting debt are created through financial ignorance. You need to get educated about how money works so all the decisions you make in the future are made intelligently. In other words, you need to be money smart.

Money Smart

The following are websites that can assist you as a teenager in developing your financial knowledge and being more money smart:

- www.moneysavingexpert.com/tips has many tips on how you can save money on loans, credit cards, insurance etc. The site is run by Martin Lewis.

- www.pfeg.org is a website dedicated to education and teaching resources for young people.

- www.whataboutmoney.info is the Financial Services Authority's guide to finances for young people.

- www.direct.go.uk/en/YoungPeople/Money is a site dedicated to providing financial help for young people.

I have a few money smart tips myself which are as follows:

- Earlier we discussed the APR (the total annual percentage rate) in relation to credit transactions. This is important as it shows how your total debt is calculated and how much extra you stand to repay on the amount you have borrowed.

  The APR is the rate that is charged to you by a bank (or any other financial institution) on the amount you have borrowed over a one year period. The rate includes simple interest on the principal amount borrowed, plus other fees and charges. This then translates into an APR.

  For example if you borrowed £2000 for one year and the interest and other fees total £360, the APR would be 18%, or 1.5% monthly (1.5% x 12 months = 18%)

- The rule of 72 applies for your debt also; your interest charge can double over 6 years also depending on how high your interest charge is.

- To get a good return of interest you must shop around.

- Always pay your bills on time as arrears on cards, overdrafts and loans attract interest, and on other bills may even end up in court fines, which in turn may end up damaging your credit rating.

A word of warning, particularly to older teenagers going to University or just starting work! As soon as you open your first account you will receive offers of a loan, new credit card, extended overdraft or credit zone facilities.

Not just your bank manager but also credit card companies, loan companies; everyone is going to want a part of the new you and unless you are disciplined and stick to the financial principles which you have learnt in this book, you are going to end up in debt and out of control financially.

Not everyone is going to like you making sensible choices about how and where you spend your money.

RULE 5

51% of teenagers said they would like to learn how to control their spending...

Develop A Financial Mindset
Action/Attitude

The purpose of this book is to develop your financial education so that you have a positive, knowledgeable and healthy attitude towards financial matters.

Did you know that Richard Branson who is now a billionaire started his own business at 16 years of age? Or that Bill Gates who is one of the richest men in the world dropped out of University in his late teens and set up Microsoft when he was just 20 years old? Mark Zuckerberg was studying at Harvard University when he had the idea for facebook. Many other well known entrepreneurs started businesses in their teens, and there is currently the highest number of teenage millionaires in existence ever (check out this link on the internet for an article on young millionaires: http://www.youtube.com/watch?v=HGbt00ms7dQ&feature=youtubegdata. There is also an ever increasing number of young people in their teens and early twenties starting internet businesses and making vast fortunes.

So as you can see, developing the right attitude to managing your money at an early age is really important to your financial future.

A good way to develop your understanding of financial matters is to read books on finance. The fact that you are reading this book shows that you have a good start but I would recommend that you read more, and here are some books that might interest you:

1. The Richest Man in Babylon by George Clason

2. Guide to Student Money by Gwenda Thomas

3. Rich Dad Poor Dad for Teens by Robert T Kiyosaki and Sharon L. Lechte

These publications and others will help you develop a wider understanding of personal finance matters and money management techniques.

If you start from now and consistently manage your money according to these rules I can guarantee that you will have a successful financial future.

NOTES

Five Rules to manage your money at whatever age you are:

1. Never spend more money than you have

2. Save, save, save!

3. Avoid getting into debt

4. Educate yourself financially

5. Develop a financial mindset

CHAPTER 4
MONEY MANAGEMENT FOR UNIVERSITY STUDENTS

If you're thinking of going to University a whole new set of financial challenges await you as you move from teenager to young adult.

The recent announce announcement by the Government that University Fees could more than treble to £9,200 is once again a reminder of just how expensive higher education is in Britain today.

There is the very real possibility that students will be leaving University with debts larger than those incurred by their parents in purchasing their first house!

In addition to the above, there is evidence that students are struggling with debt, not only during the course of, but also after the completion of their studies. A recent survey (Times Newspaper 18 August 2009) suggested that students starting university this year could end up with debts of £23,000 or more after graduating.

Student debt is no joke and is becoming increasingly serious. So what can be done about it? Well here are the Ant's top ten tips for surviving your degree with as little debt as possible:

1. **Live at Home** – A substantial part of student expenditure goes on living and eating expenses when living away from home. Accordingly, If at all possible stay at home, this way you can save rent, save the cost of meals, washing, drying and utility bills. I appreciate this is not ideal university experience but it can be just as much fun. However, I would not suggest that you actually choose your University for this reason, <u>but as the above report makes clear it will increasingly become a factor in your choice.</u>

2. **Student discounts** – There are endless discounts for students to make your lives easier in terms of expenditure, including travel, clothing, cinema, restaurants and portswear, to name a few. Your NUS card is a gateway to numerous discounts (see www.nus.org.uk) but also check out the following sites, some of which offer not only discounts but free stuff including cash. www.studentdiscounts.co.uk, www. studentbeans.com, and www.wealthystudent.co.uk

3. **Check your bank account** – It is a well known fact that the first bank a student chooses to open an account with is probably the one

that he or she will stay with long after their education has been completed (I stayed with Nat West for about 18 years after I had completed University). The banks are well aware of this fact and therefore bend over backwards to secure student accounts. You must use this to your advantage and make sure you carefully examine the bank account you pick as a student. There are numerous incentives given by banks to try and secure you as a customer but you must choose your bank based on sound financial criteria such as overdraft facilities, interest and account charges rather than free gifts. I do not personally recommend any particular account but suggest you check out websites such as www.moneysupermarket.com/current**accounts/** and **www.moneyfacts.co.uk/banking/.../banking_stud_accounts.**

4. **Cook your own food** – Whether living at home or in student accommodation you can save money on your lunch and dinners by cooking your own food. Eating out (even in halls of residence) for lunch and dinner can eat into your limited funds and can be avoided by cooking your own meals and taking them as packed lunch to University.

5. **Get a job** – Many students work their waythrough university by using part time income to supplement grants and student loans. Obviously you should ensure that work does not intrude on your studies to the point where it becomes counter- productive but if you can balance part time working and

studying it can not only provide you with extra income but also help you to start saving for your post university life.

6. **Bursaries** – Another means of supplementing your grant or student loans is applying for a bursary. Bursaries are given by universities or colleges to eligible students. English universities and colleges that charge fees over £2,835 are obliged to provide extra financial help to students on a low income who receive the full Maintenance grant or special support grant. Check out www.studento.com for a guide to bursaries.

7. **Buy and sell second hand books** – You don't need to spend hundreds of pounds per year on new text books. You can buy second hand books from students who have just completed the academic year of you degree or course you are entering. The advantage of buying such books is that they are probably annotated and have the important provisions already highlighted. You should however check that the books you are buying are not out of date. You can also buy second hand books online. Checkout **www.sellstudentbooks.com** and **ww.academicbooktrade.co.uk**

8. **Mentoring /Student Ambassadors-** All universities need student ambassadors who offer tours around the campus to prospective students and assist during events. Some Universities also have connections with local schools and need student mentors to work with school children. All the positions are paid

and are on a casual basis. If you find yourself short on money being a student ambassador can help you bring in a bit of extra cash when it's needed without you having to make a weekly commitment.

9. **Online** – As can be seen above, the internet is an invaluable source of information on how students can save money. Use the internet to research any questions you have on finances relating to student loans, bank accounts, discounts, eating out and living away from home.

In conclusion, remember the years you spend in higher education are supposed to be amongst the most rewarding and exciting time of your life, don't let debt ruin it.

CHAPTER 5

We started with the Ant so lets finish with it and look at some of its attributes that will greatly assist you on your journey to financial wholeness:

1. **It prepares for winter while it is summer** – The Ant practices storing up for hard times, in other words it saves. As we have seen this should be a part of any successful financial strategy.

2. **Its eyes are on the future** – When it comes to money you must be future focused like the Ant. The steps in this book will help you take those steps but, only if you are willing to make the difficult decisions for your long term financial future.

3. **It has the ability to delay gratification** – If you don't have the patience to wait and curb your expenditure while you are young and developing your strategy you will mess up your financial future. The Ant takes the resources it

collects in the summer and moves it towards winter. Will somebody else show up to do it for the Ant? No! Are there predators looking for an opportunity to steal what the Ant has got? Yes, but it's so focussed it doesn't have time to worry about predators.

4. **It has a cause bigger than itself** – The Ant regularly takes on and tries to move food which is considerably larger than itself; it is not just providing for itself but also for members of its colony. The financial decisions you make are often not only for your now but also for your future. When you make your decisions always keep in mind the bigger picture.

I sincerely hope that this book has helped you in developing your understanding of how money operates in our society and how you can manage it to your best advantage.

NOW PASS THIS BOOK TO YOUR PARENT(S), OR GUARDIAN!!

CHAPTER 6
A NOTE TO PARENTS

As parents today, raising children and teenagers in the consumer driven 21st century is a nightmare. The media, peer pressure, branded sportswear, mobile phones, PS3, Wii, and X Box all scream the same thing at our youngsters again and again, Spend! Spend! Spend! Children and teenagers are a goldmine for all the big companies seeking to expand their markets in search of new customers and guess who is paying? Yes it's the parents!!

As parents, guardians or custodians, it's your duty to make your children aware of their responsibility for money at an early age.

So how do we as parents cope in this environment and try to instil in our children sound financial values today?

1. **It's never too early to learn** – Children learn very early that money is important. Christmas money, birthday money, money from Aunties,

Uncles and God Parents, and then there is the bank of Mum and Dad. So if that's the case teach children early that money is not to be wasted, it's to be treated with respect and it doesn't just "come out of a hole in the wall" as my 6 year old daughter once told me. Help your children understand that sometimes the money is just not there so they can't have everything they want.

2. **Teach your child how to budget** – For most children/teenagers money is for spending, and once they get it that's what they do. Clothes, cinemas, going out with friends, trainers, and computer games. As parents you need to teach your children the basics of money management and that starts by teaching them to budget. Now, I don't mean a full blown spread sheet, but the basics; **save a little spend a little** even as children will go a long way towards setting the basis of understanding financial management.

3. **Teach the value of money** – As children get older we need to teach them the value of money. For a start, there is no such thing as "**something for nothing**". It needs to be understood that there is a relationship between money and effort. Just as parents go to work for money so children/teenagers need to exert effort to obtain financial reward. Encourage your children to do chores for their pocket money, and your teenagers to get a part time job. This is the way the real world works; you are not doing your children any

favours by leading them to believe otherwise.

4. **Teach the value of saving** – As above it's never too early to teach your children to start saving. Indeed Parents should also start saving almost as soon as the child is born. If you can, put child benefit into a long term savings account or take some of that Christmas and Birthday money and put it away for later on. School and university fees don't come cheap and you don't want to get caught having to take out numerous loans just to get your child an education.

5. **Teach financial education** – Unfortunately one of the major deficiencies of our education system is that it does not prepare children for financial management. So most young people don't understand how the world of finance works; they don't understand credit, debt, what is the best student account, the best saving accounts. Prepare your teenagers for financial reality or they will find out too late that it's much easier to get into debt than it is to get out. There are lots of books you can buy that teach both children and teenagers about finance but perhaps the best way to teach is for you to take your children with you when you're banking or paying your bills, so they can learn from you.

6. **Teach self-sufficiency** – Your teenager wants those jeans, trainers, that game, that outfit? Well let them find 50% and you as parents pay the other half. Teenagers need

to learn to contribute to their outgoings like their mobile phone bills instead of expecting parents to pay for them, and parents need to encourage their children to meet their fair share of outgoings instead of just agreeing to pay for everything.

In conclusion, as parents we need to do everything possible to teach our children how the world of money works; the sooner they understand it, the sooner they can start making responsible decisions which will benefit both themselves and their parents.

Other titles from the Author:

Go to the Ant ISBN No: 978-1907402012

Contact: **Paramount Inc Limited**, 19 Leyburn Road, Edmonton, London, Edmonton, London N18 2BG

Website: **www.gototheant.co.uk**

Email: **mail@gototheant.co.uk**

Facebook: http://www.facebook.com/pages/Go-to-the-Ant/106216012748330

ASPIRE TO INSPIRE BEFORE YOU EXPIRE

Unknown............

GO 2 THE ANTZ!

www.ingramcontent.com/pod-product-compliance
Lightning Source LLC
Chambersburg PA
CBHW071037080526
44587CB00015B/2654